WORDS FROM THE WISE

PARENTING WITH PROVERBS

LEADER'S GUIDE

DEANA CERNIGLIA

iUniverse, Inc.
New York Bloomington

Words From the Wise/Parenting With Proverbs
Leader's Guide

Scriptures taken from the Holy Bible, New International Version®, NIV®. Copyright © 1973, 1978, 1984 by Biblica, Inc.™ Used by permission of Zondervan. All rights reserved worldwide. www.zondervan.com

iUniverse books may be ordered through booksellers or by contacting:

iUniverse
1663 Liberty Drive
Bloomington, IN 47403
www.iuniverse.com
1-800-Authors (1-800-288-4677)

ISBN: 978-1-4502-6491-4 (sc)
ISBN: 978-1-4502-6492-1 (ebook)

Printed in the United States of America

iUniverse rev. date: 10/13/2010

Leader's Guide

Words From the Wise/ Parenting With Proverbs shows readers how to use the timeless words of wisdom from the Book of Proverbs to tackle tricky parenting tasks, maintain sanity and strengthen a nurturing relationship with the Father. Cerniglia offers solid guidance, tips and strategies to conquer even the most difficult challenges of parenting. She explains that in order to be a good parent, readers must analyze themselves to avoid passing down any hurts or dysfunctional behaviors learned from their own childhood.

Based on the personal experience of a mother with three children, this guide uses humor, stories, and a friend-to-friend approach that acknowledges all parents make mistakes. ***Words From the Wise*** demonstrates how readers can apply a traditional value system to today's dilemmas, showing that God's way is the best way.

Dear Leader,

Thank you for taking on this responsibility and equipping the people in your class with His Wisdom, His Word. It is so important to learn how God wants us to raise His precious creation. It is the most important job on the planet but parenting is not often viewed in this light. I'm so happy that this book is being shared in a group setting- parents need to vent and share, that's the only way we know "we're not the only ones".

If this is a teen parenting class, I am even more excited! Having been raised by a 17 year old, single mother, I know the challenges that they face and some of the youthful mistakes they will make, due in part to what has been passed down to them! By the grace of God my mother and I have healed our pasts and our relationship and I want to share His grace with your class!

We need to equip young mothers with the tools they need to raise their children. When we utilize His Word, we make healthier choices, creating healthier relationships.

On the other hand, if this is not a teenage-pregnancy class, you are still in good hands! We all need His guidance in raising our children! I share many of the mistakes I made in a friend-to-friend dialogue. We need to feel united, therefore, I am very candid and honest about the trials of parenthood.

The purpose of this class is multifaceted!

1. To lead your class to the Heavenly Father who heals our past so that we don't pass it down to our children!

2. Equip your class with His wisdom, love and grace, so they CAN pass it down to their children.

3. Share His perfect ways of parenting.

4. To HEAR your clients, provide a safe place to share concerns, fears and frustrations without judgment.

How the program works!

1. Reading the book is a must! Stress the importance of following through, God works through discipline and passion! Encourage your class to take this opportunity and use it to their fullest!

2. The workbook will probe some sensitive areas, encouraging your class to think about their past, who they are and who they want to be. Stress the importance of doing the work! It will benefit their life and the life of their child by learning all the areas of parenthood and self-discipline.

3. And last but not least, the Proverb sheets that you will do in class. I want to emphasize the importance of these proverbs! These words of wisdom will help your clients learn about how the Word of God relates to their life, which is not what the workbook does! The workbook helps your class to learn more about who THEY are and the proverb sheets is their link in learning who their CREATOR is!

4. Copy/revise the syllabus so your class is equipped with the lay out of the class. Go through the guide to get acquainted with the program. There is a class sheet (instruction guide) for the leader for EVERY class and there is a proverb sheet (student) for every class except the first class- the first class is utilized for getting to know one another. This will give your class the ability to read the material for the following week.

Now that I've said my peace, this is just a "guide", a guide of suggestions. I encourage you, the leader, to take and leave as much of my "guidance" as you'd like and tailor this to the needs of your class. The Holy Spirit has led you to lead this class and there will be different aspects He will put on your heart, follow them, make it unique, his creation was meant to be creative!

I pray that you will be His light and His seed that will be planted and take root.

Many Blessings,

Deana Cerniglia

Class 1: Get to Know One-Another!

Suggestions:

1. Stress the importance of this class, use your Leader's Guide as guidance.

2. Read the first paragraph of my Acknowledgements in the book. This sentiment is written to my mother, it is also written to your client. See what kind of reaction you get, let them talk about how it makes them feel, encourage them to talk about their emotions and allow them to share their story. Some of these women have never been "heard", they've been told what to do, scolded for what they've done and have not found a soft place to land. Acknowledge and praise them for choosing life.

3. If this is not a class for teen moms, have your class share how many children they have, their ages and what they are hoping to get out of class.

4. Read the Dear Reader together. This takes a light-hearted turn, it is funny, relatable and written in a friend-to-friend dialogue. This may spark your teen's interest to follow through with the whole class or give your mommy group time to relate with their own stories. Open up discussion with some of your own questions!

5. Make copies of the syllabus on the following pages and hand out in class. Run through the syllabus together, letting them feel that you are taking this journey together.

6. Words From the Wise/Parenting with Proverbs

Syllabus

<u>Class 1</u>
Get to know one-another!
This week: Read Chapter 1 pgs. 1-12
Do Workbook: 12 questions for reflection pgs. 7-10

<u>Class 2</u>
Discuss Chapter 1 pgs. 1-12
This week: Read Chapter 1: Inventory 1 & 2 pgs. 12-21
Do Workbook pgs. 11-14

<u>Class 3</u>
Discuss Chapter 1: Inventory 1 & 2
This week: Read Chapter 1: Inventory 3 & 4 pgs. 21-32
Do Workbook pgs. 15-20

<u>Class 4</u>
Discuss Chapter 1: Inventory 3 & 4
This week: Read Chapter 1: Inventory 5 & 6 pgs. 30-41
Do Workbook pgs 21-24

<u>Class 5</u>
Discuss Chapter 1: Inventory 5 & 6
This week: Read Chapter 2: Staying Organized, pgs. 42-46
Do Workbook pgs. 25-26

Class 6
Discuss Chapter 2: Staying Organized
This week: Read Chapter 2: Boundaries, pgs. 46-50
Do Workbook pgs. 27

Class 7
Discuss Chapter 2: Boundaries
This Week: Read Chapter 2: The Enemy on the Screen, pgs. 54-59
Do Workbook pgs. 29

Class 8
Discuss Chapter 2: The Enemy on the Screen
This week: Read Chapter 3: Mt. Everest, Eating Habits pgs. 60-73
Do Workbook pgs. 31-32

Class 9
Discuss Chapter 3: Eating
This week: Read Chapter 3: Mt. Rushmore, Discipline pgs. 73-102
Do Workbook pgs. 33-35

Class 10
Discuss Chapter 3: Discipline
This Week: Read Chapter 3: Kilimanjaro, Got Sleep? Pgs. 102-109
Do Workbook pgs. 37-39

Class 11
Discuss Chapter 3: Sleep
This Week: Read Chapter 4: Job Description: Parents of the Human Race pgs 110-122
Do Workbook pgs. 41-42

Class 12
Discuss Chapter 4: Job Description: Parents of the Human Race
This week: Read Chapters 5 & 6- they are short, pgs. 123-130

Do Workbook pgs. 43-44

<u>Class 13</u>
Discuss Chapter 5 & 6 and anything else that is concerning your journey ahead!

Dear Leader,

Copy the proverb worksheet following each class guide for your class. Each group will get one. They will use these proverbs from the readings to come up with their own interpretation of how to apply the proverbs to the different life skills.

This will encourage them to think about God's Word and how it applies to their life and to all the topics covered in the chapters. In addition, they will feel more comfortable brainstorming in a group and sharing the responsibility of answering "correctly".

Allow 10 minutes for each group to complete the sheets then go around the class and cover each proverb, one at a time.

Give them positive feedback!

Class 2: Chapter 1: How Full Is Your Well

1. Discuss text pgs. 1-12 and workbook pgs. 7-10. To begin dialogue, share one answer of your own. Discuss 15-30 minutes.

2. Break into small groups. Have your groups do the Proverb sheets and emphasize the topic: How would you apply the following proverbs to your relationship with God?

3. Give them 10 minutes to write down their answers and go around the room, sharing the different responses.

Class 2 Chapter 1 How Full is Your Well pgs. 1-12

Proverbs 14:15
A simple man believes anything, but a prudent man gives thoughts to his steps.

Proverbs 26:11
As a dog returns to its vomit, so a fool repeats his folly.

Proverbs 22:3
A prudent man sees danger and takes refuge, but the simple keep going and suffer for it.

Proverbs 25:19
Like a bad tooth or a lame foot, is reliance on the unfaithful in times of trouble.

Class 3: Chapter 1 Inventory 1 & 2

1. Discuss book pages 12-21, God is speaking- are you listening? Even if you're not married, what does the book say to you about marriage? What have you learned? Is it different from what you have in your belief system? Touch on workbook pgs. 11-14.

2. Break into small groups and do the proverb sheet. Emphasize the questions: How would you apply the proverbs to: Listening to God and Marriage?

Class 3 Chapter 1 Inventory 1 & 2 pgs. 12-21

Apply these proverbs to listening to God:
Proverbs 8:10-11
Choose my instruction instead of silver, knowledge rather than choice gold, for wisdom is more precious than rubies, and nothing you desire can compare with her.

Proverbs 16:1
To man belong the plans of the heart, but from the Lord comes the reply of the tongue.

Apply these proverbs to your marriage:
Proverbs 18:9
One who is slack in his work, is brother to one who destroys.

Proverbs 17:27
A man of knowledge uses words with restraint, and a man of understanding is even-tempered.

Class 4: Chapter 1 Inventory 3 & 4

1. Discuss book pages 21-32 and workbook pages 15-20. Choose a few questions that match your class and discuss as a group.

2. Break into small groups and do proverb sheets, emphasize relating proverbs to ego and money. Share the answers one group at a time.

Class 4 Chapter 1 Inventory 3 & 4 pgs. 21-32

Relate these proverbs to ego:

Proverbs 18:8

The words of a gossip are like choice morsels; they go down to a man's inmost parts.

Proverbs 20:27

The lamp of the Lord searches the spirit of a man; it searches out his inmost being.

Relate these proverbs to money:

Proverbs 10:15

The wealth of the rich is their fortified city, but poverty is the ruin of the poor.

Proverbs 12:11

He who works his land will have abundant food, but he who chases fantasies lacks judgment.

Class 5: Chapter 1: Inventory 5 & 6

1. Discuss text pages 32-41 and workbook pages 21-24. Suggestion: Ask the class to share a God-given personality trait that will help them in the journey of parenthood.

2. Break into groups and do proverbs sheet. Remind your class to focus on how these proverbs relate to self-discipline and personality.

Class 5 Chapter 1 Inventory 5 & 6 pgs. 32-41

Relate these proverbs to self-discipline:
Proverbs 16:26
The laborer's appetite works for him; his hunger drives him on.

Proverbs 15:19
The way of the sluggard is blocked with thorns; but the path of the upright is a highway.

Relate these proverbs to personality:
Proverbs 22:6
Train a child in the way he should go; and when he is old he will turn from it.

Proverbs 10:9
The man of integrity walks securely; but he takes crooked paths will be found out.

Class 6 Chapter 2 Molehills: Staying Organized

1. Discuss text pgs. 42-46 and workbook pgs. 25-26. Ask your class what they thought of this chapter. Do they think setting staying organized is relevant to parenting? Have them share one area in their life where they stay organized.

2. Break up into small groups and do proverb sheet. Remind the class that the emphasis on the proverbs is boundaries.

Class 6 Chapter 2 Molehills: Staying Organized pgs. 42-46

Relate these proverbs to staying organized, being diligent.
Proverbs 13:4
The sluggard craves and gets nothing but the desires of the diligent are fully satisfied.

Proverbs 20:4
A sluggard does not plow in season; so at harvest time he looks and finds nothing.

Proverbs 24:30-31
I went past the field of the sluggard, past the vineyard of the man who lacks judgment; thorns had come up everywhere, the ground was covered with weeds, and the stonewall was in ruins.

Proverbs 10:17
He who heeds discipline shows the way to life, but whoever ignores correction leads others astray.

Class 7 Chapter 2 Molehills: Boundaries

1. Discuss book pgs. 46-54 and workbook pg. 27. Ask the class if they have a boundary that is a deal breaker. In other words, they will not tolerate.

2. Break into groups and do proverbs sheet. Remind the class that the emphasis is on boundaries.

Class 7 Chapter 2 Molehills: Boundaries pgs. 46-54

Relate these proverbs to setting boundaries with children:

Proverbs 25:28 Like a city whose walls are broken down, is a man who lacks self-control.

Proverbs 30:15 The leech has two daughters, "Give,give" they cry.

Proverbs 8:12 I wisdom, dwell together with prudence; I possess knowledge and discretion.

Proverbs 22:3 A prudent man sees danger and takes refuge, but the simple keep going and suffer for it.

Class 8 Chapter 2 Molehills: Enemy on the Screen

1. Discuss book pgs. 54-59 and workbook pg. 29. Ask your class if they've given thought about what they watch and how it affects them.

2. Break up into small groups and do proverb sheet. Point out the emphasis is on media and what the world is trying to "feed" us.

Class 8 Chapter 2 Molehills: Enemy on the Screen pgs. 54-59

Relate these proverbs with the enemy on our televisions and computers:
Proverbs 4:25-27
Let your eyes look straight ahead, fix your gaze directly before you. Make level paths for your feet and take only ways that are firm. Do not swerve to the right or the left, keep your foot from evil.

Proverbs 7:21-22
With persuasive words she let him astray; she seduced him with her smooth talk. All at once he followed her like an ox going to the slaughter.

Proverbs 16:17
The highway of the upright avoids evil; He who guards his way, guards his life.

Proverbs 12:6
The words of the wicked lie in wait for blood, but the speech of the upright rescues them.

Class 9 Chapter 3 Mountains: Mt Everest: Healthy Eating

1. Discuss book pgs. 60-73 and workbook pgs. 31-32. Ask your class one thing they learned about healthy eating habits.

2. Break into small groups and do proverb sheet. Emphasize that the focus is on eating and what we put into our "temples".

Class 9 Chapter 3 Mountains: Mt. Everest: Healthy Eating pgs. 60-73

Relate these proverbs to eating:

Proverbs 22:28
Do not move an ancient boundary stone set up by your forefathers.

Proverbs 9:1-2
Wisdom has built her house; she has hewn out its seven pillars, she has prepared her meat and mixed her wine; she has also set her table.

Proverbs 4:20-22
My son, pay attention to what I say; listen closely to my words. Do not let them out of your sight, keep them within your heart; for they are life to those who find them and health to man's whole body.

Proverbs 6:23
For these commands are a lamp, this teaching is a light, and the corrections of discipline are the way to life.

Class 10 Chapter 3 Mountains/Mt. Rushmore: Discipline

1. Discuss book pgs. 73-101 and workbook pgs. 33-35. Ask your class how they were disciplined and what they want to take with them and what they want to leave behind.

2. Break up into groups and complete proverbs sheet. Be sure to emphasize the proverb is to be related to how our Heavenly Father views discipline.

Class 10 Mountains Mt. Rushmore: Discipline pgs. 73-101

Relate these proverbs to disciplining your child:

1. Proverbs 22:6 Train a child in the way he should go, and when he is old he will not turn from it.

2. Proverbs 23:13-14 Do not withhold discipline from a child, if you punish him with the rod, he will not die. Punish him with the rod and save his soul from death.

3. Proverbs 30:17 The eye that mocks a father, that scorns obedience to a mother, will be pecked out by the ravens of the valley, will be eaten by the vultures.

4. Proverbs 29:1 A man who remains stiff-necked after many rebukes will suddenly be destroyed- without remedy.

5. Proverbs 27:23-24 Be sure you know the condition of your flocks, give careful attention to your herds; for riches do not endure forever, and a crown is not secure for all generations.

Class 11 Chapter 3 Mountains/ Kilimanjaro: Got Sleep?

1. Discuss book pgs. 102-109 and workbook pgs. 37-39. Ask your class

2. Break into small groups and complete proverb sheet. The proverb emphasis is on the importance of our God –given role as parents.

Class 11 Chapter 3 Mountains/ Kilimanjaro: Sleep pgs. 102-109

Relate these proverbs to getting your child to sleep:

1. Proverb 12:24 Diligent hands will rule, but laziness ends in slave labor.

2. Proverb 26:13 As a door turns on its hinges, so a sluggard turns on his bed.

3. Proverb 20:18 Make plans by seeking advice; if you wage war, obtain guidance.

4. Proverb 13:4 The sluggard craves and gets nothing, but the desires of the diligent are fully satisfied.

Class 12 Chapter 4 Job Description: Parents of the Human Race

1. Discuss book pgs. 110-122 and workbook pgs. 41-42.

2. Break into small groups and complete proverbs sheet. The proverb emphasis is on our God-given responsibility of parenthood.

Class 12: Chapter 4 Parents of the Human Race pgs. 110-122

Relate these proverbs to stay-at-home vs. "having it all":

Proverbs 1:20-21 Wisdom calls aloud in the street, she raises her voice in the public squares; at the head of the noisy streets she cries out, in the gateway of the city she makes her speech.

1. Proverbs 1:15 My son, do not go along with them; do not set foot on their paths.

2. Proverbs 14:1 A wise woman builds her house; but with her own hands the foolish one tears hers down.

3. Proverbs 28:19 He who works his land will have abundant food, but the one who chases fantasies will have his fill of poverty.

4. Proverbs 17:1 Better a dry crust with peace and quiet, than a house full of feasting with strife.

Class 13 Chapters 5 & 6: Keeping the Self/ Living in This World

1. Discuss book pgs. 123-130 and workbook pgs. 43-44. Ask your class if they have a support system in place. Offer suggestions, such as a local church, i.e., Mom's day out!

2. Break up into groups and do last proverb sheet. Proverb emphasis is on our relationship with God, filling our well, and living in this world but not being OF this world.

3. Give your well wishes, ask if there are any questions that the materials did not cover.

Thank you Leader! And God Bless you!

Class 13 Chapters 5 & 6 Keeping the Self/ Living in This World pgs. 123-130

Relate these proverbs to refreshing oneself:

1. Proverbs 18:24 A man of many companions may come to ruin; but there is a friend who sticks closer than a brother.

2. Proverbs 29:21 If a man pampers his servant from youth; he will bring grief in the end.

3. Proverbs 27:18 He who tends a fig tree will eat its fruit, and he who looks after his master will be honored.

Living in This World:
4. Proverbs 27:11 Be wise my son and bring joy to my heart, then I can answer anyone who treats me with contempt.